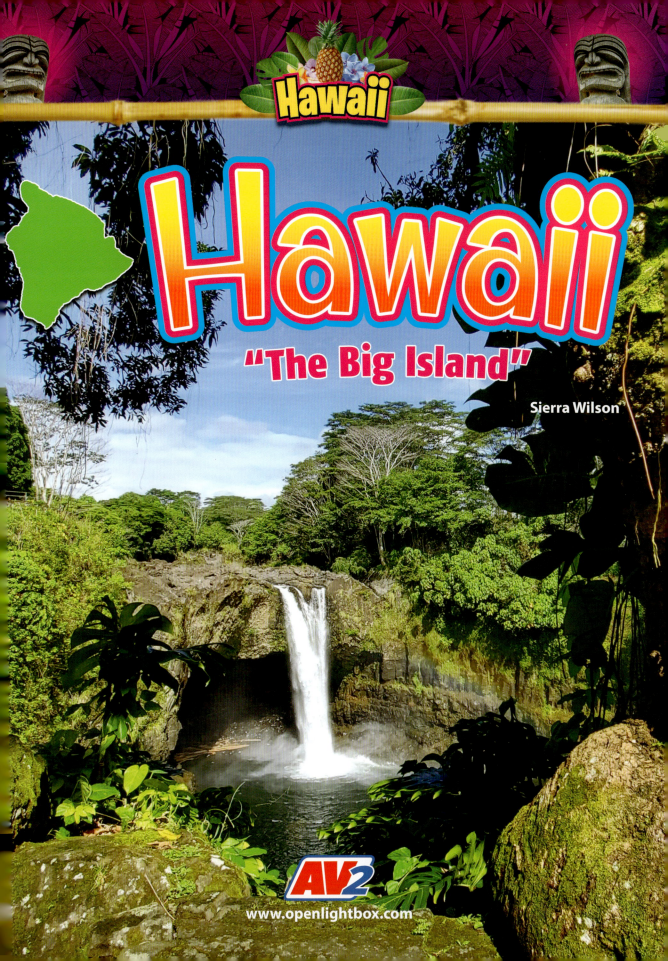

Step 1
Go to www.openlightbox.com

Step 2
Enter this unique code
OJPBGQ3VX

Step 3
Explore your interactive eBook!

CONTENTS
4 Welcome to Hawaii
6 Beginnings
8 People and Culture
10 Exploring Hawaii
12 Land and Climate
14 Plants and Animals
16 Places to See
18 Things to Do
20 Looking to the Future
22 Quiz Yourself on Hawaii

AV2 is optimized for use on any device

Your interactive eBook comes with...

Contents
Browse a live contents page to easily navigate through resources

Audio
Listen to sections of the book read aloud

Videos
Watch informative video clips

Weblinks
Gain additional information for research

Slideshows
View images and captions

Try This!
Complete activities and hands-on experiments

Key Words
Study vocabulary, and complete a matching word activity

Quizzes
Test your knowledge

Share
Share titles within your Learning Management System (LMS) or Library Circulation System

Citation
Create bibliographical references following APA, CMOS, and MLA styles

This title is part of our AV2 digital subscription

1-Year Grades K–5 Subscription
ISBN 978-1-7911-3320-7

Access hundreds of AV2 titles with our digital subscription.
Sign up for a FREE trial at www.openlightbox.com/trial

The digital components of this book are guaranteed to stay active for at least five years from the date of publication.

Hawaii
"The Big Island"

CONTENTS
- 2 Interactive eBook Code
- 4 Welcome to Hawaii
- 6 Beginnings
- 8 People and Culture
- 10 Exploring Hawaii
- 12 Land and Climate
- 14 Plants and Animals
- 16 Places to See
- 18 Things to Do
- 20 Looking to the Future
- 22 Quiz Yourself on Hawaii
- 23 Key Words/Index

WELCOME TO Hawaii

The Hawaiian Islands are located **2,390 miles** (3,846 kilometers) from the continental United States.

A flight from Los Angeles to Hawaii takes about **5.5 hours**.

Hawaii is nearly **2 times as large** as all of the other Hawaiian Islands combined.

Aloha! Welcome to Hawaii! Hawaii is the name of the largest and easternmost island in the Hawaiian **archipelago**. The Hawaiian Islands are located in the Pacific Ocean, far off the southwestern coast of the United States. They are among the most isolated areas of human population on Earth. Together, the Hawaiian Islands make up the U.S. state of Hawaii.

The island of Hawaii is nicknamed "The Big Island." This is because it is the largest of the Hawaiian Islands. Hawaii is known for its high mountain peaks and lush landscapes. It is a popular destination for travelers.

THE ISLAND OF Hawaii

Population: 208,800 (2024)

Area: 4,028 square miles (10,432 sq. km)

Altitude: 13,796 feet (4,205 meters) at its highest point

County Seat: Hilo

Island Flower: Ōhiʻa lehua

Island Color: Red

HAWAII—The Big Island

Beginnings

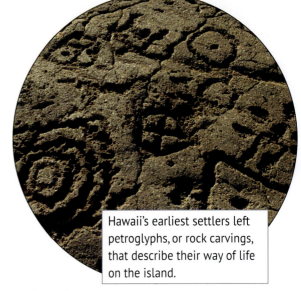

All of the Hawaiian Islands were formed by volcanic activity. Hawaii is the youngest island in the island chain. It is about 400,000 years old. The island continues to be shaped by its active volcanoes even today.

Hawaii was the first Hawaiian Island to be settled by **Polynesians**. These early Polynesians arrived between 400 and 500 AD. In 1778, English Captain James Cook arrived in the area. This marked the start of Hawaii's contact with Europe and the rest of the world. Eventually, the Hawaiian Islands came under the control of the United States, becoming a U.S. state in 1959.

Hawaii's earliest settlers left petroglyphs, or rock carvings, that describe their way of life on the island.

Native Hawaiians had been living undisturbed for hundreds of years before Captain Cook came to the islands.

Speaking Hawaiian

The word *Hawaii* means "small homeland." It is pronounced "ha-WAH-ee."

6 HAWAII

Hawaii Timeline

400–500 AD
Polynesians from the Marquesas Islands sail across the Pacific Ocean and begin settling on Hawaii.

1778
Captain James Cook and his crew arrive on the Hawaiian Islands.

1810
After years of conflict, Hawaii's chiefdoms are united under a single leader, King Kamehameha I, a warrior from the Big Island.

1819
King Kamehameha's rule of Hawaii comes to an end.

1820
Christian **missionaries** arrive on Hawaii to teach their religion.

1960
A large **tsunami** hits Hawaii, killing 61 people and resulting in more than $70 million worth of damage.

2023
Hawaii's Kilauea volcano erupts three times over the course of a year.

HAWAII—The Big Island

People and Culture

A rich blend of cultures can be found on Hawaii. The island's oldest traditions come from Polynesia. The ancient Polynesians worshiped nature-based gods. They built temples, called *heiau*, on Hawaii. The old stone walls and platforms of these temples can still be seen on the island.

Polynesian culture continues to be practiced and celebrated on the Big Island to this day. Artisans use ancient Polynesian designs and techniques to carve wooden canoes, weave mats and baskets from leaves, and string together floral necklaces called *lei*. Each Hawaiian Island has its own traditional form of lei. The lei of the Big Island is made from the red flowers of the lehua tree.

The Ahuena Heiau, in Kailua, was the personal temple of Kamehameha I. It is believed to be where he died.

Speaking Hawaiian

In Hawaiian, *lei* means "garland" or "wreath." It can be pronounced either "lay" or "lay-ee."

Dance is another important part of Polynesian culture. Hawaiian hula dancing began as a part of religious ceremonies. The different dance moves in hula help to tell stories about battles, gods, and nature. Hula dancers study in *halau* dance schools for years. Hula dancing is still practiced and performed on all of the Hawaiian Islands. Top hula dancers compete at an annual festival. Along with the hula festival, there are many other festivals and events in Hawaii that celebrate Polynesian culture each year.

Polynesian fire dancing is another cultural dance seen in Hawaii. It is often performed at Hawaiian *luaus*, or feasts.

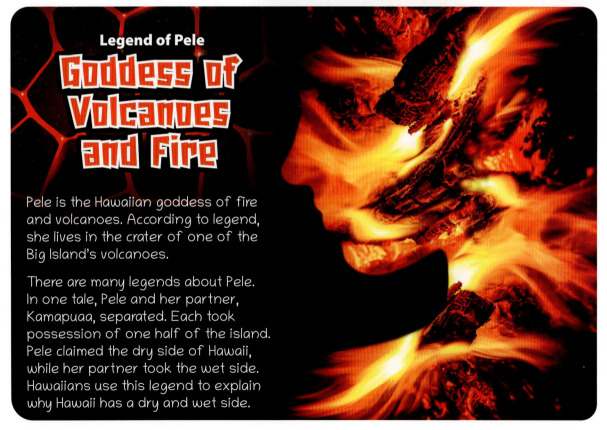

Legend of Pele
Goddess of Volcanoes and Fire

Pele is the Hawaiian goddess of fire and volcanoes. According to legend, she lives in the crater of one of the Big Island's volcanoes.

There are many legends about Pele. In one tale, Pele and her partner, Kamapuaa, separated. Each took possession of one half of the island. Pele claimed the dry side of Hawaii, while her partner took the wet side. Hawaiians use this legend to explain why Hawaii has a dry and wet side.

HAWAII—The Big Island 9

Exploring Hawaii

As the largest of the Hawaiian Islands, Hawaii takes up 63 percent of the state's land. Its size provides the island with a variety of features and many interesting places to see. People visiting the island of Hawaii can view deep valleys, dramatic waterfalls, and long beaches.

Hilo
Hilo is the island of Hawaii's business center. Its deep-water port allows for the export of orchids, pineapples, macadamia nuts, and cattle from the island.

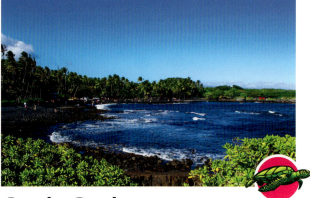

Punaluu Beach
Punaluu Beach is a black sand beach on Hawaii's southeast coast. The beach is a popular spot to see green sea turtles. They often come ashore there to catch some sun.

Kailua-Kona
Kailua-Kona served briefly as Hawaii's ancient capital under King Kamehameha I. Tourists in Kailua-Kona can visit Hulihee Palace, which is now a museum, and other historic buildings.

Akaka Falls
Akaka Falls is a 442-foot (135-m) tall waterfall within Akaka Falls State Park. It is one of the tallest waterfalls in Hawaii. It can be reached via a short hiking trail.

Waipio Valley

The Waipio Valley is a popular place for tourists who want to see beautiful views. From the valley lookout, tourists can see tropical plants, beaches, and mountains.

Kealakekua Bay

This bay is a protected marine **sanctuary** known for fish, sea turtles, and coral. It is also where Captain James Cook was killed during a conflict with the locals. Today, the bay features a monument to Cook.

HAWAII—The Big Island

Land and Climate

Perhaps the most impressive features on Hawaii are its mountains. The island is home to the tallest mountain in the world, if measured from its base beneath the sea. Mauna Kea is about 33,500 feet (10,210 m) tall from the seafloor up. That is 4,400 feet (1,340 m) taller than Mount Everest.

Some of Hawaii's mountains are especially notable because they are active volcanoes. Hawaii is home to four of the six active volcanoes in the Hawaiian Islands. The island's most active volcano is Kilauea. It has erupted frequently throughout the past 40 years and is covered in lava flows. Another important volcano on Hawaii is Mauna Loa. It is the largest active volcano on Earth.

Hawaiians consider Mauna Kea to be the most sacred of all the archipelago's volcanoes. It is believed to be the home of many Hawaiian gods.

Speaking Hawaiian

The word *mana*, pronounced "mah-nuh," means "spiritual power." According to Hawaiian beliefs, sacred places have great mana. Many Hawaiians consider volcanoes sacred.

12 HAWAII

Hawaii is a unique island because it is home to nearly every type of climate found on Earth. The island has climate zones ranging from wet tropical areas to polar tundras. Some places are quite sunny, while others are usually rainy.

Average High Temperatures

JAN	81°F (27 °C)
FEB	81°F (27 °C)
MAR	82°F (28 °C)
APR	82°F (28 °C)
MAY	83°F (28 °C)
JUN	85°F (29 °C)
JUL	86°F (30 °C)
AUG	87°F (31 °C)
SEP	86°F (30 °C)
OCT	86°F (30 °C)
NOV	84°F (29 °C)
DEC	82°F (28 °C)

Tropical storms can bring strong winds, high waves, and flooding to Hawaii, creating dangerous situations for people living there.

HAWAII—The Big Island

Plants and Animals

With its variety of climate zones, Hawaii is home to many different types of plants and animals. Some are found only on the island. Others are found throughout the Hawaiian archipelago.

Hawaiian Hoary Bat

The Hawaiian hoary bat is the only land mammal that is native to Hawaii. These bats roost in trees during the day and hunt at night. They eat insects such as mosquitoes, moths, and beetles. Hawaiian hoary bats are considered to be **endangered**.

Uhiuhi

Once found throughout the Hawaiian Islands, the uhiuhi now grows only on Hawaii, Kauai, and Oahu. This tree is mostly found on mountainsides, where it can reach heights of more than 30 feet (9 m). The uhiuhi can be recognized by its pink or red blooms.

Mauna Kea Silversword

The Mauna Kea silversword is an endangered plant found only on the upper slopes of its namesake mountain. The plant is known for its silvery-green leaves and purple blooms. It can grow up to 9 feet (2.7 m) in height.

Green Sea Turtle

The most common sea turtle in Hawaii is the green sea turtle, or *honu*. One of the best places to spot these turtles is along Hawaii's Kona Coast. Here, they feed on seaweed in bays and reefs. They also visit local beaches to lay their eggs.

Humpback Whale

Humpback whales spend each winter in Hawaii. They travel all the way from Alaska to mate and give birth in warmer waters. They can often be spotted off the Big Island's west coast. These majestic animals can reach lengths of 60 feet (18 m) and weigh up to 40 tons (36 metric tons).

Hawaiian Hawk

The Hawaiian hawk is the only hawk found on the Hawaiian Islands, and it lives only on the island of Hawaii. These birds are typically found in forests, where they feed on insects, rodents, and other birds. The Hawaiian hawk was once a symbol of Hawaiian royalty.

HAWAII—The Big Island

Places to See

Hawaii is a popular tourist destination, with a wide variety of interesting places to visit. Hawaii Volcanoes National Park is a must-see on the island as it includes two active volcanoes. Visitors can see steaming craters and even walk through a 600-foot (183-m) long **lava tube**.

Another popular tourist site is Mauna Kea. People often visit the top of the volcano at night to admire the stars in the clear sky above. There are several telescopes and **observatories** at the top of Mauna Kea. Stargazing guides and tours are also available.

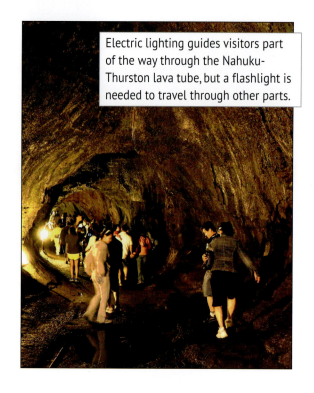

Electric lighting guides visitors part of the way through the Nahuku-Thurston lava tube, but a flashlight is needed to travel through other parts.

Scientists from around the world come to Mauna Kea to study distant galaxies from the mountain's many observatories.

To get a glimpse into Hawaii's ancient past, tourists can visit the Puako Petroglyph Archaeological Preserve. The preserve has more than 3,000 petroglyphs carved into lava rock. The petroglyphs date back to 1200 AD and show human figures, canoes, sea turtles, and other shapes.

Trails through Puako Petroglyph Archaeological Preserve allow visitors to see approximately 1,200 of the site's carvings.

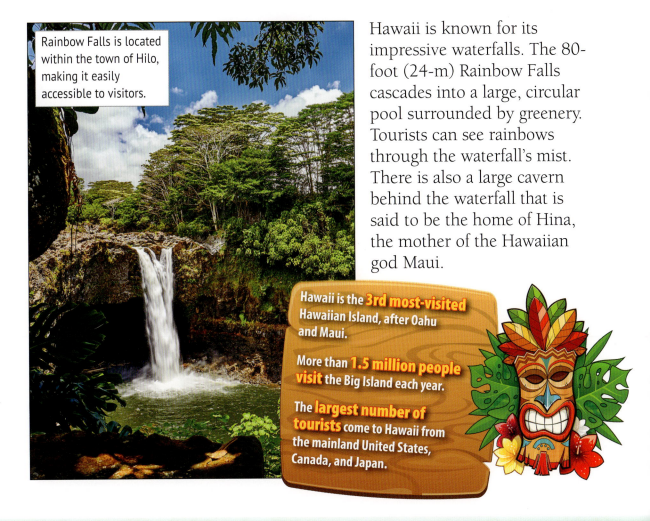

Rainbow Falls is located within the town of Hilo, making it easily accessible to visitors.

Hawaii is known for its impressive waterfalls. The 80-foot (24-m) Rainbow Falls cascades into a large, circular pool surrounded by greenery. Tourists can see rainbows through the waterfall's mist. There is also a large cavern behind the waterfall that is said to be the home of Hina, the mother of the Hawaiian god Maui.

Hawaii is the **3rd most-visited** Hawaiian Island, after Oahu and Maui.

More than **1.5 million people visit** the Big Island each year.

The **largest number of tourists** come to Hawaii from the mainland United States, Canada, and Japan.

HAWAII—The Big Island

Things to Do

With mild weather and a wide variety of natural features, Hawaii is ideal for the outdoor enthusiast. Many people come to the island to go snorkeling. Hawaii has an abundance of ocean life and 266 miles (428 km) of coastline. Tourists can snorkel on their own or join guided tours to see a broad array of colorful sea creatures. For a special experience, visitors can go snorkeling at night with manta rays.

The crystal-blue waters around the Big Island make it one of the best places in Hawaii for snorkeling.

Another popular water activity in Hawaii is surfing. Hawaii has areas that are suited to all skill levels. Beginners can sign up for surfing lessons from local surf schools and learn how to catch waves.

Hawaii's beaches are often less crowded than those on Oahu or Maui, allowing surfers to have more waves to themselves.

Speaking Hawaiian

Heenalu, pronounced "heh-eh-nah-loo," is the Hawaiian word for "surfing." While surfing is a recreational activity today, ancient Hawaiians saw it as a ritual. Surfing was a way of praying to the gods.

18 HAWAII

Exploring Hawaii's waters can also be done by boat. Between November and April, visitors can take whale watching tours to see humpback whales up close. Dolphins sometimes make an appearance as well. They will often follow boats and jump in their **wake**.

Scientists estimate that between 10,000 and 12,000 humpback whales make the journey from Alaska to Hawaii every year.

For people wanting to experience the land, Hawaii has several ranches that offer guided horseback tours. Some popular areas for horseback riding include the Hamakua Coast, Waipio Valley, and near Waimea. Tourists can also explore Hawaii's landscape by hiking or riding all-terrain vehicles.

Hawaii is known for its cowboy culture. Horseback tours allow Hawaii's *paniolos*, or cowboys, to share their way of life with guests to the island.

HAWAII—The Big Island

Looking to the Future

Living on a tropical island, with its warm weather and beautiful scenery, can seem like the ideal life. However, island life comes with its challenges. Hawaiians, like all Hawaiian Islanders, are trying to navigate through these issues and find solutions.

Tourism contributes greatly to Hawaii's **economy**. While the island needs this income, it is struggling to handle the increasing number of people coming to visit. Aging **infrastructure**, such as roads and buildings, needs to be updated and improved to handle more people. Some of this work is in progress, but it is creating its own problems. Road construction causes even more traffic congestion. New hotels displace residents and damage the environment.

In 2024, Hilo received $17.5 million to improve several of its roadways so that the city can accommodate more traffic and improve flow. It had been years since previous upgrades had been done.

HAWAII

Wildlife can become caught in debris that washes onto beaches. They may also ingest it, thinking it is food. Either action can cause serious harm to the animal.

SPOTLIGHT on CHANGE

Volunteers and staff with the Hawaii Wildlife Fund remove 15 to 20 tons (14 to 18 metric tons) of garbage from the beaches and waters around Hawaii and the other Hawaiian Islands each year.

Removing this waste helps protect sea animals and ocean environments. However, it is important that waste be either reduced, reused, or recycled. What are some ways to achieve each of these goals?

Visitors can also cause more direct problems for the Big Island. As an island, there are only so many ways for its people to dispose of trash. Visitors do not always respect the rules in this regard. They leave trash on beaches and in parks. This can harm the island's wildlife and the **ecosystems** they rely on. To protect the environment, officials are working to educate tourists about proper trash disposal. Local groups also organize community clean-ups.

HAWAII—The Big Island   21

QUIZ YOURSELF ON Hawaii

1 What is the Hawaiian name for the green sea turtle?

2 How long is Hawaii's coastline?

3 How many people visit the Big Island every year?

4 What is the island flower of Hawaii?

5 What is the name of the largest active volcano on Earth?

6 When did the island of Hawaii begin to form?

7 Which Big Island city once served as Hawaii's ancient capital?

8 When did Hawaii become a U.S. state?

ANSWERS: 1. Honu **2.** 266 miles (428 km) **3.** More than 1.5 million **4.** Ohia lehua **5.** Mauna Loa **6.** About 400,000 years ago **7.** Kailua-Kona **8.** 1959

22 HAWAII

Key Words

archipelago: a group of islands

economy: the wealth and resources of a country or area

ecosystems: communities of living things that share an environment

endangered: in danger of no longer living on Earth

infrastructure: the basic facilities and systems serving a country, city, or area, such as transportation, power plants, and schools

lava tube: an underground passage formed by the flow of lava

missionaries: members of religious groups that are sent into an area to promote their faiths

observatories: buildings that hold large telescopes for observing the stars and planets

Polynesians: people from a group of Pacific islands called Polynesia

sanctuary: a place where someone or something is protected or given shelter

tsunami: a giant wave caused by earthquakes or volcanic eruptions under the sea

wake: the track of waves left by a ship or other object moving through the water

Index

Akaka Falls 10, 11
animals 10, 11, 14, 15, 21

climate 12, 13, 14
Cook, Captain James 6, 7, 11

dance 9

environment 20, 21

gods and goddesses 8, 9, 12, 17, 18

Hilo 5, 11, 10, 17, 20
horseback tours 19

Kailua-Kona 10, 11, 22
Kamehameha I 7, 8, 10
Kealakekua Bay 11

lei 8

Mauna Kea 12, 15, 16

Pacific Ocean 5, 7, 11
plants 5, 8, 11, 14, 15
Polynesians 6, 7, 8, 9
Puako Petroglyph Archaeological Preserve 17
Punaluu Beach 10, 11

snorkeling 18
surfing 18

tourism 10, 11, 16, 17, 18, 19, 20, 21

volcanoes 6, 7, 9, 12, 16, 22

Waipio Valley 11, 19
whale watching 15, 19

HAWAII—The Big Island 23

Get the best of both worlds.

AV2 bridges the gap between print and digital.

The expandable resources toolbar enables quick access to content including **videos**, **audio**, **activities**, **weblinks**, **slideshows**, **quizzes**, and **key words**.

Animated videos make static images come alive.

Resource icons on each page help readers to further **explore key concepts**.

Published by Lightbox Learning Inc.
276 5th Avenue
Suite 704 #917
New York, NY 10001
Website: www.openlightbox.com

Copyright ©2026 Lightbox Learning Inc.
All rights reserved. No part of this publication may be reproduced, stored in a retrieval system, or transmitted in any form or by any means, electronic, mechanical, photocopying, recording, or otherwise, without the prior written permission of the publisher.

Library of Congress Cataloging-in-Publication Data

Names: Wilson, Sierra, author.
Title: Hawai'i "the Big Island" / Sierra Wilson.
Description: New York, NY : Lightbox Learning Inc., 2026. | Series: Hawaii | Includes index. | Audience: Grades 2-3
Identifiers: LCCN 2024047330 (print) | LCCN 2024047331 (ebook) | ISBN 9798874506544 (library binding) | ISBN 9798874506551 (paperback) | ISBN 9798874506568 (ebook other) | ISBN 9798874506582 (ebook other)
Subjects: LCSH: Hawaii Island (Hawaii)--Juvenile literature.
Classification: LCC DU628.H28 W55 2026 (print) | LCC DU628.H28 (ebook) | DDC 919.69/1--dc23/eng/20241211
LC record available at https://lccn.loc.gov/2024047330
LC ebook record available at https://lccn.loc.gov/2024047331

Printed in Guangzhou, China
1 2 3 4 5 6 7 8 9 0 28 27 26 25 24

122024
101124

Project Coordinator: Heather Kissock
Designer: Terry Paulhus

Photo Credits
Every reasonable effort has been made to trace ownership and to obtain permission to reprint copyright material. The publisher would be pleased to have any errors or omissions brought to its attention so that they may be corrected in subsequent printings. The publisher acknowledges Getty Images, Alamy, Shutterstock, and Wikimedia as its primary image suppliers for this title.

View new titles and product videos at www.openlightbox.com